GOLF LES-
SONS FROM
SAM SNEAD

GOLF LES-SONS FROM SAM SNEAD

Bailey Campbell

Hawthorn Books, Inc.
Publishers
New York

FOREWORD

THIS book grew out of a real need to put in hard cover form, where golfers of all abilities could use it permanently, simple, workable tools for playing good golf. But as any golfer knows, the skill does not come out of a book. However, instruction can. Repeated in frequent lessons—and with much practice—the instruction can lead to most successful results.

This necessary reference guide is now available. It can serve the highly skilled golfer who may be off his game, or the beginner who is doing so many things wrong that he does not know where to start to improve his faults.

In this particular series of lessons, an eighteen-handicapper (at the time) goes to the Master for help in performing a weekend variety of a game he loves—and yearns to play well.

From tee to green, from fairway to trap, the author moves smoothly and easily through a series of dialogues— six lessons—by trial and error, to an improvement that is almost instant. But this step forward is just that first step and demands constant application if the first lessons are to pay off.

And what more practical means for golf improvement is there? Lessons from the man who has Everything, as far as golf is concerned, Sam Snead. Bailey Campbell, a Florida advertising executive, swings right into the first lesson, with little or no preamble. Snead, in turn, pulls no punches in telling him what he does wrong. We recommend that you engage in the Snead-Campbell dialogue, which follows immediately—and improve yourself!

The Editors

CONTENTS

1. Grip, Stance, and Power

"WHAT'S your handicap?" asked Sam Snead.

"Eighteen," I said.

"Take your seven-iron and let me see you hit the ball."

I pulled the club out of my bag and addressed the ball nervously, trying to remember all the how-to-do-it tips I had ever read about the game. Then, putting my best swing forward, I hit a beautiful shot about a hundred and fifty yards straight down the middle!

"Eighteen, my foot!" Sam exclaimed.

A few shots later I was back on my game, and Sam started to work on me.

"You've got the idea now," Sam said. "What you've got to do is practice. I want you to get out on the practice range for a couple of hours before your next lesson."

And that was my first lesson at the Boca Raton Hotel and Club from Samuel Jackson Snead, the man with the sweetest swing in golf.

"You know one of the main reasons 99 per cent of golfers are dubs? It's in their grip," drawled Sam. Then he showed me how to hold the club using the Vardon, or overlapping, grip. My grip was pretty good except for two things. First, Sam told me I was gripping the club too tightly. Of all that I learned in this first lesson, I believe this advice was the most helpful.

The basic Vardon (overlapping) grip

Second, he pointed out that it is extremely important to develop a sense of "feel" in the grip.

To demonstrate just how lightly the club should be gripped, Sam, facing me, grabbed my lower right forearm. He held it with about the same amount of pressure you would use in holding a bird, just firm enough not to let it fly away, but not firm enough to hurt it. I had read conflicting opinions on this point, but I soon realized that Snead feels a light grip is essential to a fluid swing and maximum power at impact.

"It's sort of like hitting a baseball," he told me. "If you squeeze the bat to death and use all your power throughout the swing, you put less power into the ball at contact. You want to let that power go when you hit the ball. You not only hit it farther, you swing smoother, because you're relaxed."

The proper grip is essential to good golf. Grip the
club gently but firmly.

"To put it another way, if I throw a punch like this [Sam tightened the muscles in his arm, drew straight back, and shot his tensed arm forward], I haven't got much of a blow. But if you bring your arm back, co-ordinate your body into the blow, and then let your power go at contact, with the weight of your body behind it, you're throwing a Sunday punch. Same thing happens in the golf swing.

"Remember this, it's not how *hard* you hit the ball that counts; it's *how* you hit it. That's why so *many* little guys can hit the ball farther than the big guys."

Proper body co-ordination will result in a naturally powerful golf swing.

On the subject of "feel," Sam emphasized proper positioning of, and pressure from, the right thumb and forefinger on the golf club handle. The right thumb is placed just left of the center of the shaft. It is extended, and light but firm pressure is applied by the ball of the thumb to the shaft. This pressure is felt in the second joint of the right forefinger. Pick up a club and try it. Once you get the idea, you can see how proper positioning and pressure from these two fingers provide "touch" from club control.

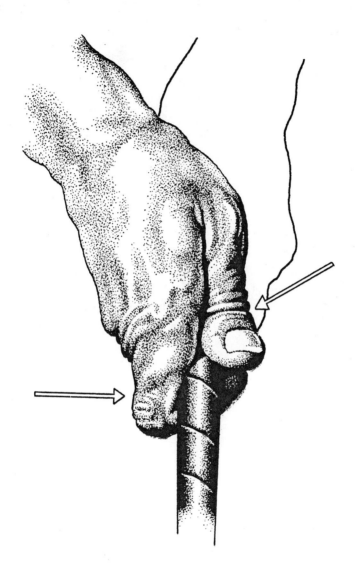

The pressure of the right thumb and forefinger will produce the proper "feel" in your grip.

Since almost every average golfer knows what the Vardon grip is—how the little finger of the right hand overlaps the forefinger of the left—Sam didn't elaborate on this. However, he did stress the importance of keeping the hands together and never letting them part from start to finish.

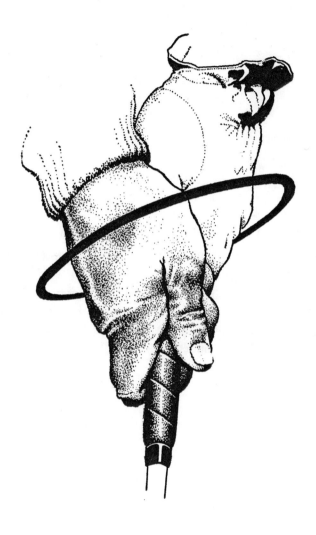

Hands must stay together from the start to the finish
of the swing.

I always felt that a tight grip was necessary to keep the club face from opening at impact.

"That's for the birds," said Sam. "Your grip will automatically tighten at the proper time on the downswing, helping to throw the clubhead into the ball so that you get maximum power at impact."

Hands automatically tighten on the down swing to give you maximum power at impact.

I'll try to tell you how it felt the first time I tried a light grip the way Sam told me. In addressing the ball and holding the club without a lot of pressure, it seemed inevitable that the club would turn in my hands when it made contact with the ball. Ignoring this apprehension, I took the club back in the normal manner, then down and through the ball. I knew instantly that my swing was more relaxed and smoother. All tension was gone. My grip automatically tightened on the downswing. I got that good feeling that comes when the wrists uncock at just the right moment. There was a crisp sound as the club made contact. As Sam said, "I can tell a good shot without seeing it. All I have to do is hear the crack of the ball."

He had me hit some more balls. And, believe me, what he said really worked. I was hitting five, six, and seven shots in perfect succession.

The complete golf swing

Then I goofed. Encouraged by my improved perform-ance, I raised my head, dug the face of the club into the ground, and the ball rolled out about thirty yards.

"You let me watch where the ball is going; you just hit it," Sam said. "Your job is to concentrate on good contact with the ball, not where it's going."

Of course, we all know that, but as Sam says, "You'll al-ways be a dub if you don't concentrate on the basic funda-mentals of the game."

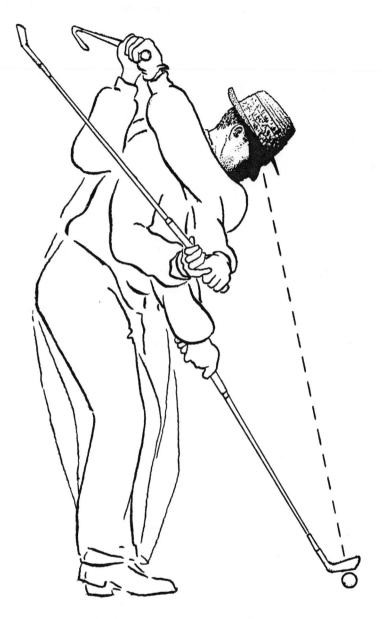

KEEP YOUR EYES ALWAYS ON *THE TEE*
THROUGHOUT THE SWING.

After he felt I was beginning to hit the ball with a better grip and sense of feel, he went to work on my stance. It seems that I was crouching over the ball a little too much. I had a tendency to bend too much at the waist, letting my hands fall down with an exaggerated break at the elbows.

"If you crouch too much, you will naturally straighten up at impact," Sam noted. "This change of position throws you off balance and interrupts your swing. Not only that, but if you don't extend your arms at address, you shorten the radius of your swing. This means you lose power, because usually the wider the arc of the swing, the more clubhead speed you get at impact."

INCORRECT STANCE: Note the crouch and exaggerated break at the elbows.

Sam took the club and assumed the proper stance. First he looked toward his target. Then he placed the clubhead behind the ball. Finally, he positioned his feet. He bent slightly in the waist, and his knees were flexed.

"I can always tell a good golfer when he approaches the ball," he pointed out. "Just watch the pros. They never position their feet and then the clubhead. You've got to put the clubhead behind the ball where it will naturally be at the bottom of the downswing and at the point of contact. Then you bring your feet into place."

CORRECT STANCE: This stance will give you maximum power in your swing.

"Another thing. Play the ball near the center of your stance on all short irons—never back of center on normal shots. Sometimes when you need more loft to get over trees you should play the ball slightly forward. And if you want to play a low shot, place the ball slightly back of center. But for all normal shots play from a center line between your feet."

Ball position is extremely important when shooting for the green.

After making these corrections in my stance, he had me hit some more balls. I was doing better, no doubt, but then I began pulling the ball to the left.

"You're locking your right leg on your backswing then," Sam said. "Remember, you've got to keep both legs flexed and relaxed throughout the swing. This keeps the turn smooth and gives you more power. And another thing, never let your body move laterally during the swing. You cannot swing smoothly if you sway because you will have to adjust your swing to compensate for the sideways movement of your body. You should feel as if you're standing in a barrel. When you make a full turn you revolve inside the barrel.

"Ever play football?" Sam asked.

"A little," I said.

"Did you play in the backfield?"

"Quarterback," I answered.

"Well, on a hand-off or spinner play remember how your knees were flexed so that you could turn right or left and keep perfect balance? The same thing applies in the turn of the golf swing. Never let either leg lock or stiffen. Keep them relaxed and slightly flexed. That's the only way you'll ever develop a smooth swing and power."

I hit another dozen balls and we called it a day.

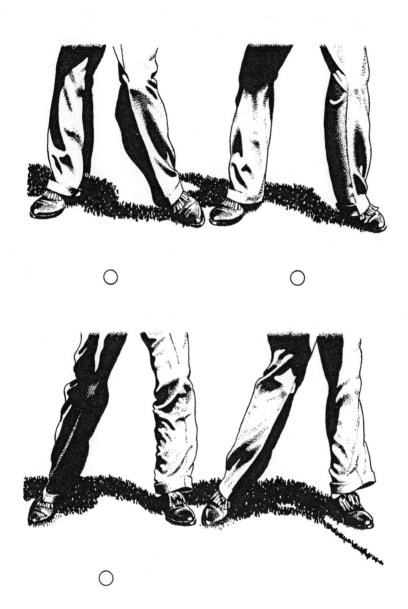

Flexed knees throughout the swing will give you a
smooth turn and more power.

2. Relax, Relax, Relax

IT'S one thing to be a great pro; another to be a good teacher. Sam Snead is both.

After a little practice and work on the fundamentals of the grip and stance, I was hitting the ball better. The over-all relaxed grip with slight pressure between the right thumb and forefinger on the shaft gave me some feel of control. I could definitely see evidence of improvement after one lesson.

In our second session I graduated from the seven to the five iron. Same grip, same stance, same positioning of the ball (on a line midway between the right foot and the left foot), same swing—relaxed, smooth, and fluid.

I hit a few balls, then Sam snapped: "What are you doing, chopping wood? Bring that clubhead back low along the ground. When you lift the clubhead on the back swing, you've thrown yourself out of position and you have to compensate on the way down. Your timing and your swing is thrown off.

"And you're locking the right leg again. Remember, both legs have to be flexed and relaxed all the way through. This is the only way you can co-ordinate your arms, legs, and body into a sweet, smooth golf swing."

It's difficult to break old habits. Locking that leg had become almost second nature with me.

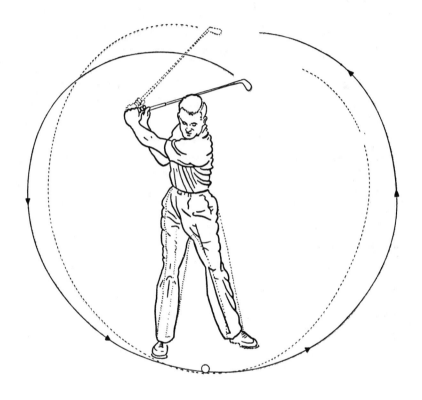

Compare the proper leg positioning and swing arc
(solid lines) with "chop" swing and "locked" knees
(dotted lines).

"Maybe this will help," Sam said. "Flex both knees slightly. Now get a little knock-kneed. That's it, point your knees inward slightly, but keep them relaxed. Now, hit another ball."

It worked. Now I've found that if I can remember to bring my knees slightly together, I have no tendency to tighten up with the right leg.

"When the pros are off, you know what's wrong ninety-nine per cent of the time?" I shook my head. "Bad leg action," Sam replied. "All parts of the body have to work together. You can't hit that ball right if your legs are working against you."

Funny, but when you swing right, you hit the ball right. You can feel it, all the way from the heels of your feet to the tips of your fingers.

"Now don't tighten up that grip," Sam warned. "Relax, relax, relax. Step up to that little ball like you're going to love it. Keep saying, 'You little sweet thing, I'm not going to hurt you.' Save all that energy and power until you need it, at the time your clubhead moves into the hitting area. Just concentrate on what you're doing. Get loose as a goose. Approach the ball gently and relaxed. Stay relaxed. Don't worry; you'll throw on the power automatically at the right time. Try to see the clubhead strike the ball."

When approaching the ball, feel and act relaxed.
The club will take care of the rest.

The pieces were beginning to fit together. I was hitting the ball better. And then I began to slice. I couldn't understand why. I had always been a hooker.

"I'll tell you why," Sam said. "You're loosening your grip at the top of the swing. The handle of the club is slipping out from under your left thumb. Let me show you what happens when you do this." In slow motion, Sam started his swing and loosened his grip at the top. On the downswing, the shaft had slipped out of position. He held the end of the shaft between the thumb and the palm instead of between the pad under the thumb and the palm. This caused the club face to be open, turned to the right of the target, at impact.

"Remember what I told you about the grip," Sam cautioned. "The hands must work together; never let them come apart. You grip the club lightly, but firmly enough to maintain your grip throughout the swing, and I mean all the way through. This applies to every club in your bag."

That stopped the slice.

The proper pressure will develop in the swing automatically. Just remember to grip the club firmly from start to finish.

Next Sam observed that I was getting too much loft on my five-iron shots. I was not hitting down and through the ball, throwing the clubhead out toward the target as I swung through. I was finishing high, but I was not extending my arms, and the clubhead, toward the target on the follow through. I was "lifting" the ball, rather than letting the clubhead drive it forward.

Then the "Slammer" demonstrated. He took the five iron and hit the ball into the wind. It never got more than twenty feet above the fairway, and it must have carried at least 180 yards. I noticed that he took a slight divot. I was hitting the ball clean, with more of a "scooping" action.

"Another thing," observed Sam, "your elbows are too far apart at the finish. This time try to keep those elbows closer together. This will help make you hit through the ball and out toward the target."

Important emphasis should be placed on keeping the elbows close together during the swing. This will help you swing through the ball.

"Now, let's review what you've learned so far," Sam said.

"First, the grip. It should be light, but firm enough to keep the club under control at all times throughout the swing. Never let it loosen. Hands work together, never apart. Pressure between right thumb and forefinger for feel and control. Remember to hold the club as you would hold a bird—firm enough to hold it but not firm enough to hurt it.

"Second, address the ball properly. Position the clubhead first, then bring the left foot into position. Don't crouch. Bend slightly at the waist with arms well extended. Relax. Flex legs and turn knees slightly inward. Concentrate on seeing the clubhead hit the ball. Relax.

"Third, don't lock your right leg on the back swing. Feel like you're swinging inside a barrel. No body sway. Bring the clubhead back low to the ground.

"Fourth, hit down and through the ball. 'Throw' the clubhead forward toward the target after it meets the ball. Finish with the elbows close together."

3. Fitting the Fundamentals

ON the day of my third lesson I found Sam on the practice range. He was preparing for an exhibition match with Arnold Palmer, set for the next day at the Country Club in Pompano Beach.

"In a hurry?" Sam asked.

"No," I replied.

He unzipped a bag of practice balls and motioned me to a nearby bench.

"Take it easy for a few minutes while I hit these balls. Try to remember what you've learned so far and watch me."

He pulled out his five iron—the club I had used in my last lesson—and motioned the caddy to the right.

"I like to shoot at a target when I'm out here practicing. See those two palm trees out there?" He pointed to two coconut palms about fifteen feet apart and about fifty yards down the range. Their fronds almost overlapped, leaving an opening between their trunks framed by fronds at the top. "I'm going to try to put the ball through that opening."

He did just that—one shot after another—swinging with a symphony of co-ordination and power that was almost unbelievable. "Feels easy when you do it right." He grinned. "When the flight of the ball has consistent trajectory, you know your swing is consistent."

49

"Aren't you opening the face of the club when you start back?" I asked. I was sitting opposite and facing Sam as he addressed the ball.

"It just looks that way because my hands are slightly ahead of the clubhead at address," Sam explained. "If I take the club back so my left arm aligns with the shaft and the clubhead, you can see that the face of the club will return squarely to the ball," he said as he demonstrated.

Bring the clubhead back low to the ground so that
the left arm aligns with the shaft and the clubhead.

"Notice how I bring the club back low to the ground and as far as possible before the wrists begin to cock. This gives your swing a nice, wide arc. It's better not to cock your wrists at all than to lift the club up on the back swing. Just remember that your hands, arms, body, and legs should move together. And you should turn, not sway."

Every time Sam hit the ball his swing was exactly the same, rhythmical and smooth, unleashing a burst of power in the hitting area.

A smooth rhythmic motion without cocking your
wrists will result in a nice, wide arc in your swing.

"When you start the club down you have the feeling of pulling down with the last two fingers of the left hand. The left hand does the work, and the right hand comes in when you are ready to uncock your wrists. Wait as long as possible before uncocking. Save your power until it counts—at the point of impact."

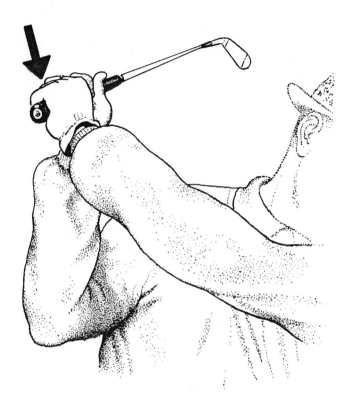

On the down swing, pull down with the last two
fingers of your left hand. The right hand will follow.

"Keep your balance on the inside of your feet. Roll your left foot inside on the back swing, right foot inside on follow through. Knees are relaxed and flexed and pointed slightly inward to keep your weight on the inside of your feet. All the time you are concentrating on what you're doing. Try to see that clubhead strike the ball. If you raise your head too soon, you won't swing through low and out. Remember, you want to try to throw that club face out along a line toward your target."

Weight balance should be kept on the inside of both feet and will vary at the different phases of the swing arc.

"Sure feels good when you do it right," Sam remarked again after he slammed one on center of target and about 180 yards out. "You've got to keep working and thinking about the basic fundamentals. Once they become second nature, you've got it whipped, but that doesn't mean you can stop thinking.

"Guess you wonder why I keep repeating the same thing over and over. Well, I'll let you in on a secret. As long as I've been playing this game, I still keep reviewing fundamentals over and over again, and sure enough, when I'm not hitting the ball right, the trouble is usually that I'm not concentrating on the very things I'm telling you."

This man is very human, I thought. At fifty-one, he is still one of the greatest players the game has ever seen, yet he's big enough to admit that he makes the same mistakes that plague dubbers like me. The difference is he doesn't make as many of them—not by a long shot!

In watching Sam, the single most impressive thing I noticed was the tremendous clubhead speed he generates at impact with the ball. I am sure this impression is heightened by the smooth and relaxed ease with which he executes the swing. Every part of his body is perfectly co-ordinated. Wasn't this what he meant when he kept repeating that I must stay relaxed and grip the club lightly and without tension, so that I would reserve the burst of power for the moment it is needed—in the hitting area?

The assimilation of all the instruction one gets in a golf lesson is a key to improving one's game. It is not until all the various fundamentals of grip, stance, swing, timing, etc., are fitted together like a jigsaw puzzle into one comprehensive pattern that one really begins to profit from instruction. As I sat there watching Sam, I could see all of these things put together in the perfect golf swing. I got a mental picture of how they worked together and a visual picture of the magnificent results.

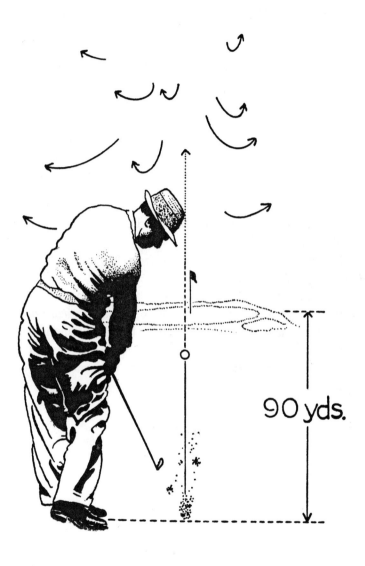

90 yds.

Even in the wind, center the ball between your feet on full short iron shots.

"Well, let's see how you can handle the three wood," Sam said.

I timidly pulled the club from my bag. It was my first try with a wood in three lessons.

"On your woods," Sam advised, "you will need more pivot on your back swing than you took with the five iron. That's because the shaft of the wood is longer, which means you swing in a wider arc. You bring the club back low, just like the irons, and you don't break that left arm, but you make more of a body turn on your pivot.

More pivot on wood shots is necessary since the shaft of a wood is longer than that of an iron and requires a wider swing-arc.

"With the fairway woods, like the long irons, you play the ball forward, just opposite the left heel in a slightly (about an inch) wider stance than with the five iron. Everything else is the same—same grip, same concentration on the ball, same follow through. You try it."

I addressed the ball, planting the clubhead squarely behind it first, then moving my feet into position.

"Loosen up! Relax! You're tighter than a bull's eyes at fly time!" Sam bellowed. Facing me he took my left forearm in his two hands and held it lightly. "Remember? I told you before that this is as tightly as you should grip the club. You've got to be relaxed. Your grip will automatically tighten up at the proper time. You just throw your swing and timing off when you get all tensed up."

I addressed the ball again.

For fairway woods, position yourself so the ball is opposite the left heel. Everything else stays the same.

"Thatta boy. Feel better?"

"Yes," I nodded, and hit the ball. It was a good ball—not like Sam's—but good and solid.

I hit several fairly decent shots in succession before I scuffed the ground behind the ball and sent it dribbling off the tee.

"Your swing was O.K., but your timing was bad. Now, don't do anything different just because you mishit the ball. Just work on your timing and repeat a smooth swing until it feels natural."

You can tell when your timing is off. But when it's right, you can actually feel those wrists uncock at the right instant with a flailing action that gives the ball a resounding crack.

"You've got to have lots of feel to get your timing right," Sam said. "And you can't get that feel if you're tightened and tensed up. Remember, nice light grip with both hands, slight pressure between right thumb and forefinger on the shaft, pull down with last two fingers of the left hand on the down swing, keeps wrists flexible, and wait until the last minute to uncock 'em."

I hit another dozen balls as well as I ever did in my life —better, in fact.

"Now, let's see," Sam mused. "We've worked on the short irons. . . . By the way," he said, "when you practice, work on the five, six, and seven irons. That's good training. Get confidence with these long clubs before you really tackle the long irons and the woods. You will groove your swing much faster that way. First two lessons we worked on the short irons. I want to save a lesson for bunker shots, one for pitching and putting, and we'll work on the woods some more."

Now you begin to "feel" your swing tempo. Wrists
uncock naturally at just the right time on the back
swing and then again on the down swing through
the follow through.

On the following day I got out on the practice range with my five iron and my seven iron while Sam matched his skill against Palmer's. It will be interesting, I thought, to see just how many strokes six lessons from Snead will take off my game.

4. Follow Through
in Sand Traps!

"THE average player's got a mental block about sand traps. Hitting out of sand isn't nearly as tough as most people think."

Sam Snead's remarks were obviously intended to give this nervous pupil some much-needed confidence. His words really hit home because for me the sand was a real nemesis.

Sam walked into the trap near the green, threw a ball on the sand, and with one smooth, almost effortless swing sent the ball sailing in a blast of sand straight toward the pin. It halted an almost perfect two feet short of the flag stick.

"The trouble with most folks," Sam drawled, "is that they're scared and they don't have the right mental attitude toward this shot. And besides this, you just can't get people to realize that you can't quit on a sand shot. Of course, you shouldn't really quit on any golf shot, but you're dead if you do it in a trap. Follow through is mighty important. If you quit, you're almost sure not to get out."

He handed me the sand wedge and told me to approach the ball. I took my usual stance, then my usual swing, and the ball only moved inches in the bunker.

"Wait a minute," he said. "Let's start from the beginning. You should open your stance a little on this shot. Play the ball forward about even with your left heel. You had it way back here, about in the center. You want to play the ball forward and open the club face slightly. Try it again, and don't forget to follow through."

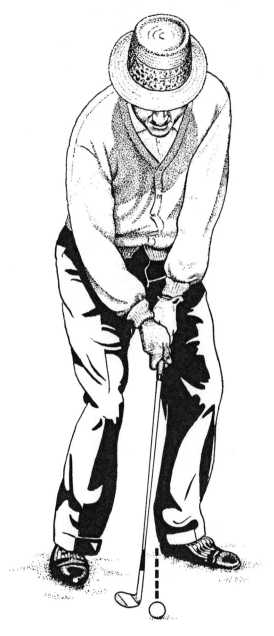

Address position of a normal sand-wedge shot

I didn't leave myself a cinch putt, but I did get out.

"You want to hit about two inches behind the ball. When you open the club face as I told you, you'll get a nice, clean, shallow cut of sand from under the ball. O.K., go ahead,

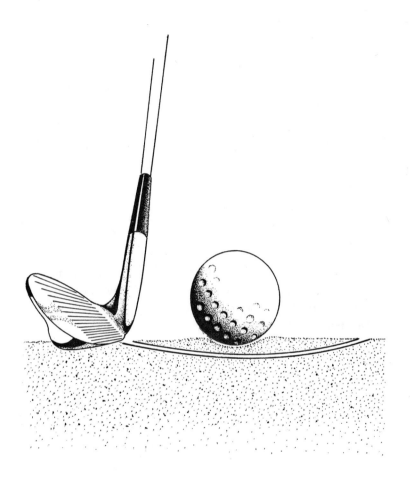

Hitting about two inches behind the ball with an
open club face will result in a shallow cut.

"Play the ball forward off the left heel, open stance, open club face slightly, and be sure to follow through." I reviewed his tips in my mind and then gave it another try. This time I did a little better.

Play the ball off your left heel, and remember always to follow through.

"When the sand is soft like this fine white sand here," he told me, "you slide the clubhead into the sand about two inches behind the ball. If the sand is firm, you hit more downward and try to take a little deeper cut. But, for Pete's sake, follow through!"

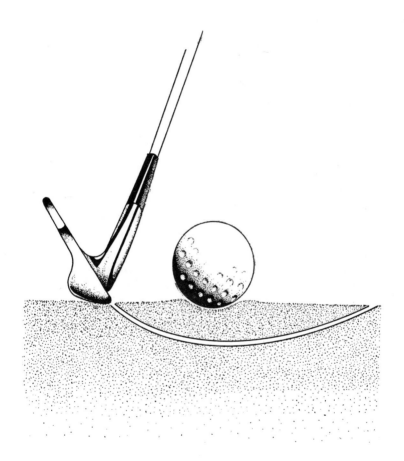

In firm sand, use a more downward swing and dig
a little deeper into the sand.

"Another thing," he warned, "be sure you have a firm footing. Get your feet into position and then wiggle them until you feel that they're firmly set in the sand. Watch any of the pros and you'll see them address the ball and do a little hula. They're getting set so their feet won't shift during the shot. This is important. Hit another one."

I did, and I was beginning to feel a little more at home in that deep bunker.

Wiggle your feet around to get a firm footing in
the sand.

"Keep the left hand firm on your back swing and pull it strongly through the sand. This will help you to keep from uncocking your wrists too soon and scooping the ball.

A firm left hand on the back swing and a strong
pulling motion on the down swing will prevent a
scooping action when hitting out of sand.

"Also, as you swing down to the ball be sure to shift your weight to the left side. There shouldn't be much shift of weight on the back swing, but there's a positive shift to the left on the down swing. This clears the hips out of the way and lets you hit down and through the ball. When you don't shift your weight to the left, it's hard to hit down and through the ball."

As the downswing progresses shift your weight to
the left side to help you hit through the sand.

This seems to be a common fault with me, not only on trap shots, but with just about every club in the bag. It's tough for me to hit down and through the ball and out toward the target. Shifting of weight to the left is essential.

"Now, let me see if I've got this straight," I said. "Address the ball and wiggle your feet to get them firmly set in the sand. Play the ball forward opposite the left heel. Stance open. Open the face of the club slightly. Not much shift of weight on the back swing, but carry the club back with a strong left hand. Don't uncock the wrists too soon. Positive shift forward to left side as you come into the ball. Hit about two inches behind it and down and through with a full finish."

"That's it," Sam said. And I said to myself, "That's it, and I wish it was as easy as Sam made it look."

"Remember that by far the safest shot out of a trap is the explosion or blast shot. Sometimes when the sand is firm and there isn't a big lip at the edge of the trap you can putt out. But there's no shot as sure and safe as blasting. You'll use the explosion shot ten to one over putting out. So, it's a good idea to practice until you've got it down pat."

"About practicing—you can't learn the game without it. No matter how skilled the teacher, after you are told what is wrong only practice will overcome faults that are almost second nature."

I was beginning to appreciate this. After my first couple of lessons from the best in the business, I saw discouragingly little improvement in my game. But consistent practice and the application of principles Sam had taught me finally began to bear fruit.

As I began to walk out of the bunker, Sam yelled, "And don't forget to follow through!"

5. "Feeling" Your Chip Shots

"WHAT'S the most important thing a golfer should develop to play a good short game?" I asked Sam Snead this question as we walked to a green for my lesson on chipping.

"A sense of feel that will give you accuracy, proper timing, and a delicate touch," Sam answered. "Now this doesn't mean that you have to chip as I do, or like any other pro, for that matter. Everybody has his own way. You play the short game the way that suits you best, but the basic fundamentals are the same for just about everybody.

"The short game is where you make or break your score," he added. "It's the hardest part of your game to learn and the first that goes bad. But still, average golfers just won't practice short shots. They'd rather bang out drives. A long ball off the tee gives you a good feeling, but it won't do as much as good chipping and putting to lower your score."

The caddie dumped some shag balls about fifteen feet from the edge of the green and Sam pulled a seven iron from the bag.

"I think this is the best club for chipping. I prefer this to a less-lofted club, say a number five, because with the seven iron's loft you will get the ball over the apron with a little backspin. I think a lot of people make a very bad mistake using a nine iron or a wedge. They usually come up short of the hole."

For chipping, a seven iron will give you more back-spin and, therefore, more accuracy.

In quick succession, he chipped three balls that carried to the green. Each time it looked as if he had overshot the hole, but the ball seemed to skid as it hit, a slight amount of backspin slowed up the roll, and none stopped more than fifteen inches from the pin.

"In playing the chip shot your feet are fairly close together, stance slightly open, with the left foot pulled back from the target line. Play the ball from opposite the center of your stance. Grip down on the club close to the bottom of the leather.

The stance and grip for the normal chip shot

"Main thing to remember is the weight on the left foot—you never shift it to the right—the weight stays on the left foot throughout the shot."

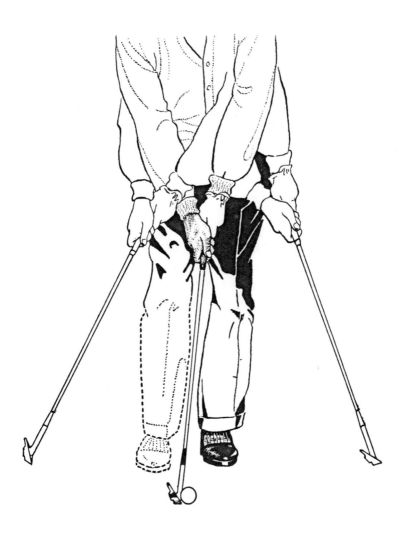

Your weight stays on the left foot throughout the
pitch shot.

"Do you use much wrist?" I asked.

"Practically none. You don't need a lot of wrist. You play it almost like a long shot. Take the club back as if it were a continuation of your left arm. Then hit down and through the ball. Don't try to loft or scoop it. The club's loft will make it rise.

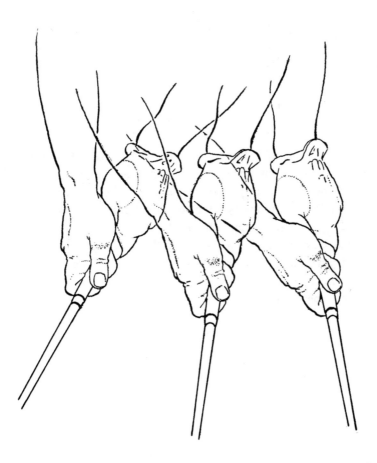

There is absolutely no wrist action throughout the chip shot.

"Try it," he said, handing me the club. "Weight on the left foot. Now hit down on the ball. See how solid that feels? See how that puts a little drag on the ball when it lands? Don't play the ball too far forward or you'll have a tendency to scoop from behind."

No question about it, chipping the ball the way Sam said gave me a firm, solid feel at impact and imparted a little backspin on the ball. I was gaining "feel." Accuracy would come with practice.

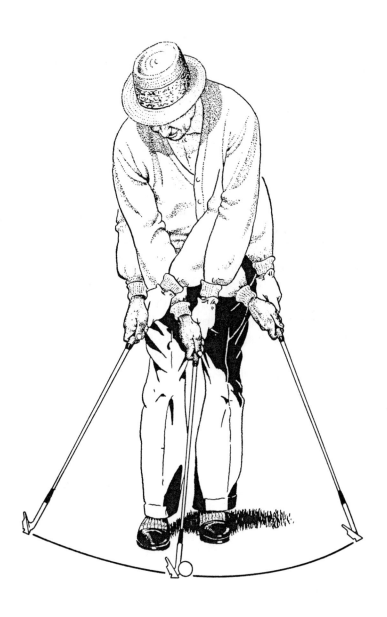

The complete chip shot

"Now don't play that ball way out where you have to reach for it. Remember, you're choking up on the club, which means you're making it shorter. So you play the ball about the same distance out as you do a putt. Another thing, when you reach for the ball you'll start weaving your body back and forth, and this ruins your accuracy. Play it up close and keep the club face looking at the target. That's better. Take the club back with both hands. Now you're getting the feel with both of your hands. That's good, you had a little more feel, didn't you? You're doing a lot better."

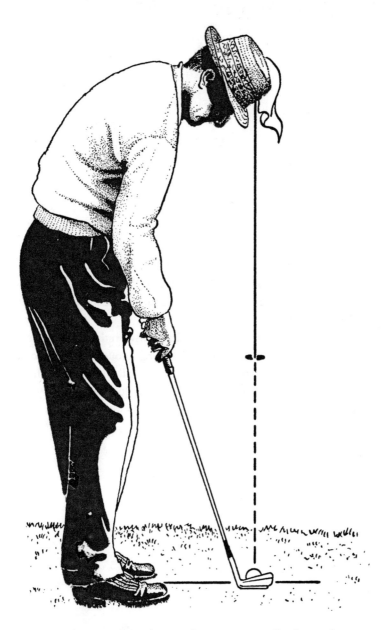

Lining up a chip shot is done very similarly to the
way you would line up a putt.

"Let me ask you something," I said. "I've read that you should chip the ball to a point about midway to the hole. Is that what you try to do?"

"I don't try to pick a spot," Sam answered. "It's the feel that's important. Just hit the ball hard enough. I could loft it up a little or keep it down. The over-all distance is what counts, and this is a matter of judging just how hard you should hit it. Concentrate on that.

over-all
distance

Concentrate on over-all distance while figuring
chipping distance.

"Now watch the position of your hands," Sam warned. "You're getting them too far forward at address. The hands should be ahead of the clubhead but never any farther than just inside the left leg.

Position your hands slightly ahead of the clubhead on all chip shots.

"You're scooping the ball again," he admonished. "That's because you're not getting your weight forward onto the left foot. Look"—he demonstrated—"when my weight isn't forward it's more natural to swing the club upward at the point of impact and in the follow through. It should move down and forward, so you get a nice, crisp contact squarely against the ball. Of all the things I have told you about chipping, this is the most important: *Keep your weight forward.*"

If you try it you'll see exactly what Sam means. Unless the weight is well forward, you don't get that solid feel at impact, and you don't have the touch that is so important to accurate distance.

"And remember to keep the club face looking toward the target," Sam warned. "Hit down and through. That's the secret."

He says you should always use the seven iron for chipping unless you have to clear a hazard, such as a trap, or when there isn't enough green to allow for roll. In these cases, the wedge is usually the club to use. By using the seven iron whenever possible you learn to feel "at home" with this club.

As the Slammer put it, "Get the feel of this club. Practice with it as much as you can. You'll find your short game will get a lot sharper, and that's what takes strokes off your game."

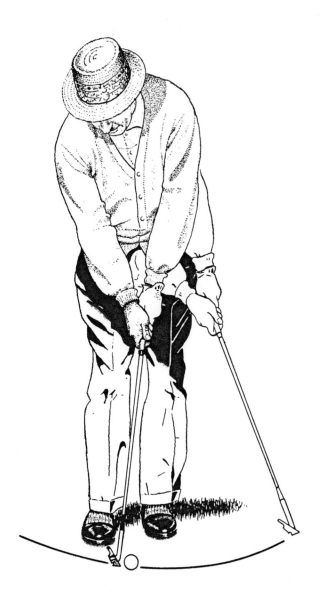

Keep the club coming through the ball rather than
on the up swing at impact.

6. Putting—
the Finishing
Touch

THE day had finally arrived when I would discover how much Sam Snead had helped me during our lesson series, and how much I had helped myself through practicing what he had taught. We had a date to play nine holes, and I met him on the putting green by the pro shop at Boca Raton.

"Before we get on the course I want to go over a few pointers on putting," Sam said.

Sam told me that on long putts you putt *to* the hole. On short ones you putt *at* the hole.

"By that, I mean you should try to finish close to the hole on the long ones, so you can always get down in two," he explained. "You'll automatically make your share of long putts, but on short putts you naturally try to hit the hole."

On a short putt, aim right *at* the hole. On a long putt, aim *to* the hole.

Sam said that it was fine for a golfer to develop his own pattern of action in putting, but he added that he felt all players should adhere to certain fundamentals. Then he demonstrated.

Sam took his stance and pointed out that his weight was mostly on his left foot.

"I don't shift any weight during my stroke," he said. "I want to keep my head and body as still as possible so that the face of the putter won't turn off line."

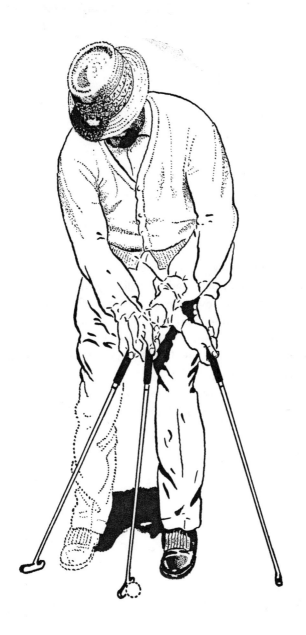

Weight is completely on the left foot when putting.

"Notice that my eyes are directly over the ball," he added, "and that my hands are slightly ahead of the ball. This gives the putt overspin as it comes off the blade. This way there is no side spin, which you get when a putt is cut or pulled. A ball struck with overspin—end-over-end rotation—will not spin off if it hits the corner of the cup. It usually will drop in.

"By all means work on keeping the blade square, or at right angles, to the take-off line of putt when contacting the ball."

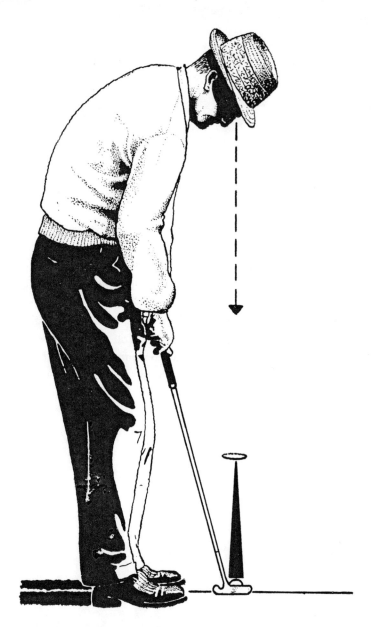

Keep your eyes directly over the ball and the blade
of the putter perpendicular to the line of your shot.

He took my putter by the grip end, held it high with the thumb and forefinger of his left hand, and tapped the blade with his right forefinger.

"First, find the sweet spot," he said. "As you tap the blade you'll find one spot that is solid. You tap it there and the putter head goes straight back without turning. That's the sweet spot. Notice exactly where that spot is and remember it."

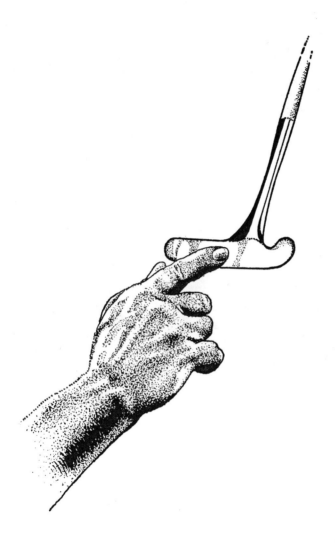

The "sweet spot" of your putter blade will give you a firm putt.

"If the hole is straightaway with no break," Sam continued, "hit the ball on the sweet spot directly toward the cup. But if you have a break from left to right, you play the ball differently."

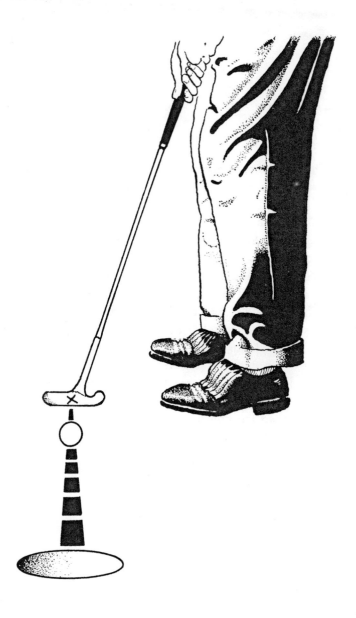

On straightaway putts, hit the ball on the "sweet spot" directly at the hole.

The green broke perceptibly from left to right. Sam approached the ball, which was about fifteen feet from the cup.

"On this shot you want to play it more forward . . . about here," Sam said, as he positioned the ball slightly forward, off his left toe.

"You have to figure out—in your mind's eye—the curved path the ball will take to the hole," he said.

"Then you take aim by placing your putter face with the sweet spot directly behind the ball and square it to the line of the ball's take-off.

"Next—to get a final idea of the speed of the putt— you look along the line the ball is to travel, then return your eyes to the ball and stroke the putt accordingly."

He stroked the ball and at first it held a fairly straight line—because he had played it from off his left toe. But, sure enough, as its speed slowed toward the last few feet, the slope of the green took effect and the ball noticeably curved on its path into the hole.

On left-to-right putts, you must gauge direction,
speed, and curve before actually hitting the ball.
Feet should be slightly more forward of the ball
than in the normal putting position.

Sam went to the opposite side of the hole and dropped a ball about fifteen feet from the cup. "If the break is from right to left, as it is from here, you play the ball back toward the center of your stance."

He squared the blade of the putter to the take-off line, with the ball exactly in front of the sweet spot, and stroked the ball on its way. This time it came to rest right at the rim of the hole.

"You can't make 'em all," Sam said, with a grin.

"Now you know how to find the sweet spot," he said. "Remember exactly where it is and stroke your putts on that spot."

On right-to-left putts, play the ball farther back than normally.

A Summary
of Sam Snead's
Basic Principles
of Golf:
How They Can
Be Put
into Action

THE GRIP: Proper grip pressure is essential to a fluid swing and maximum power at impact. Take the club in your hands with the same amount of pressure you would use in holding a bird—just firm enough not to let it fly away. Your grip will automatically tighten at the proper time on the down swing. The light grip makes the swing relaxed. Slight pressure with the last three fingers of the left hand will prevent the grip from loosening. Also apply a little pressure between the thumb and forefinger of the right hand for feel and control.

LEG ACTION: Flex both knees slightly at address. Be a little knockkneed so your weight is largely on the insides of your feet. Never lock your right leg on the back swing.

THE SWING: Bring the club back low to the ground on the take-away. This gives your swing a nice, wide arc. Remember that your hands, arms, body, and legs should move together on the take-away. And you should turn, not sway laterally, on the back swing. Keep your weight on the inside of the right foot on the back swing. Roll the left foot inside on the back swing and the right foot inside on the down swing. On the down swing pull down with the last two fingers of the left hand, lower the right shoulder and return your right elbow to your right side.

PLAYING FROM SAND: Hitting out of sand isn't as tough

as most people think. On a normal blast shot, position the ball well forward in a slightly open stance and open the club face. Try to make the wedge enter the sand about two inches behind the ball. Don't forget to follow through. CHIP SHOTS: Keep your weight on the left foot throughout the swing. Grip down on the club. Use a slightly open stance and hit down and through.

PUTTING: Keep your head and body as still as possible so the putter face won't turn off line. Putt with your eyes directly over the ball and your hands over or slightly ahead of it. This gives the ball the necessary overspin.

"C'mon," Sam said, heading for the first tee, "let's see what you've learned. Let's see if you still play like an eighteen-handicapper or if we've made some progress."

This was it. Now we would see what the old Slammer had taught a typical weekend duffer in six thorough lessons. We played the first nine, and here's how it went.

No. 1. 345 yards, par 4. I drove 240 yards but pulled an eight iron to the left of the green, leaving a wedge pitch over a sand trap. I hit the shot eight feet from the hole, and knocked in my putt for a par. I was smiling.

"You hit that putt on the sweet spot all right," Sam said, "but you wouldn't have pulled that eight iron to the left if you hadn't tightened up on the grip and tried too hard. I think you were trying to impress me," he said, laughing.

No. 2. 310 yards, par 4, a dogleg with a lake bordering the fairway on the left. I didn't hit my drive solidly, and it rolled only 140 yards. I took a three iron but hit it fat, and it stopped twenty feet short of the green. I chipped on and two-putted from ten feet for a bogey.

"You hit behind the ball a couple of times there because you swayed," Sam said. "Remember, you tilt and turn the shoulders during the swing; you don't sway back and forth."

No. 3. 382 yards, par 4. I hit a good drive, leaving myself a three-iron shot to a green well-guarded by traps. I chose to take a four iron and play safe, short of the traps. The ball stopped twenty yards short of the green, but I didn't get down in two and had to settle for a bogey five. I had fourteen strokes after three holes.

No. 4. 410 yards, par 4. I hit my drive down the middle but sliced a two wood into the right rough, about forty yards from the pin. I popped the ball out of the grass, over a trap, and it stopped on the fringe—sixteen feet from the pin. I putted for my par, hitting it on the sweet spot again, and it went in.

No. 5. 485 yards, par 5. I hit my tee shot into a fairway trap but had a clean lie and smacked a three iron about fifteen yards short of the green. I chipped with an eight iron over a bunker and the ball stopped six feet from the pin. I sank the putt for a birdie four and had twenty-two strokes through five holes—I was only one over par!

No. 6. 178 yards, par 3. I hit a four-wood shot from an elevated tee, but a wind caught the ball and carried it into a trap at the left of the green. I blasted with my sand wedge to within fifteen feet of the pin, but two-putted for a bogey four.

"That was a good sand shot," Sam said. "You didn't quit on it. Followed through just as I told you."

No. 7. 385 yards, par 4. I hooked my drive into the left rough, then hit a four wood over the green. I tried to run the ball up with a four iron, but it caught in the grass, ten feet from the apron. I chipped on with a seven iron, Sam's favorite club for chip shots, and two-putted for a bogey five. I had thirty-one strokes and was three over par.

No. 8. 150 yards, par 3. I hit a five iron off the toe of the club and landed fifty feet short of the green. I scooped my wedge shot, but it cleared a trap and came to rest on the green, twenty feet short of the pin. Then I three-putted for a double bogey five.

No. 9. 555 yards, par 5. I really caught hold of my drive and it went about 260 yards, but I topped a two wood that rolled only seventy-five yards. A better two wood put me twenty-five yards from the green and I pitched on with my nine-iron, leaving the ball twenty-five feet from the cup. I had a downhill putt over a hogback with a left-to-right break. I played it slightly forward of my left toe, as Sam advised. But I stroked it too hard and the ball rolled past the hole on the left and stopped twelve feet below the pin. Then I missed coming back, for a forty-three, seven over par.

"See what I mean about those three-putt greens," Sam drawled. "They'll kill your score. If you hadn't three-putted eight and nine you would have finished with a forty-one."

And Sam is dead right. But I'll let you in on a secret: In the four years I've been playing golf that's the best nine holes I've ever shot. I'm sure now that I'll cut quite a few strokes off that eighteen handicap, so Sam Snead's lessons certainly helped me. I hope they have helped you too.